Genre Folktale

Essential Question
Why is working together a good way to solve a problem?

The Bear Who Stole the Chinook

A Siksika Folktale

retold by Raewyn Glynn ◆ illustrated by Jeff Crosby

CHAPTER 1

Waiting for the Chinook

One year, long ago, the Siksika Indians faced the longest winter they had ever known. The freezing north wind brought sleet and hail. Deep drifts of snow buried their homes. The people waited for the Chinook wind to blow over the mountains. The Chinook would warm the air and melt the snow.

Early in the morning and in the late afternoon, the elders gathered to search the sky. "Every day, we see only heavy gray clouds," said one of the elders. "The Chinook lifts the clouds up like an arch. Where is the arch? Where is the Chinook?"

"The north wind has created many hardships for us throughout this long winter," said another.

3

"The blizzards force us to stay in our homes, but our homes are cold because we have no wood to burn. Our children are hungry, and our hunters can find no game," said a third.

As the elders stood gazing at the sky, a boy walked past them. This boy had no family and his clothes were ragged. He shared the lodge of another family, which was very crowded. For this reason, the boy spent a lot of time outside. His friends were the animals that he shared his food with.

The boy met his friends Coyote, Owl, Magpie, and Weasel in a clearing in the forest. They all agreed that the long winter had brought much suffering. "Where can the Chinook be?" said Coyote. "Magpie, see if you can find out what the chatter is," said Owl.

Magpie flew off to gather the gossip and soon returned with the news.

"Bear has stolen the Chinook!" Magpie screeched. "He wanted to stay warm all winter in his mountain home."

"That is terrible news," said Coyote.

"Everyone is afraid of Bear," said Owl, "so he thinks he can do whatever he wants.

"We must rescue the Chinook," said the boy, "or this winter will never end."

CHAPTER 2

A Rescue Attempt

The friends began the long journey to Bear's mountain den. "Magpie, you lead the way," said Weasel. "Owl and I will catch food for us all."

When night fell, the Coyote said to the boy, "Curl up next to me or you will be frozen by morning."

Four days later, the friends reached Bear's den. "Owl, you hunt at night, and your eyes are very good for seeing in the dark," said the boy. "Why don't you look through that hole in the den wall and see what you can see."

As Owl peered into Bear's den, firelight flashed in his big round eyes. Bear saw the flash of fire and jumped up. Owl could see nothing but the huge bear in front of him, growling furiously. Owl jumped back. He did not want to give himself away.

"A brave attempt, Owl," said Weasel. "But perhaps my speed is what we need."

Weasel peered into the den, then ran away as fast as she could. All Bear saw was a flash of white fur that looked like snow.

"What did you see?" said the boy.

"The Chinook is tied up at the back of Bear's den in an elk-skin bag," said Weasel.

"I have a plan," said the boy. "I always carry with me some sweetgrass and sage that I can burn to make smoke. The smoke will put Bear to sleep."

As the sweet smoke filled the den, Bear grew sleepier and sleepier until finally he was fast asleep. "Coyote, you are very quick. Why don't you creep into the den and grab the elk-skin bag," said Magpie.

In no time at all, Coyote came out carrying the bag in his strong jaws.

CHAPTER 3

Freeing the Chinook

"I have the bag," said Coyote, "but Bear has tied it very tightly. It will not be easy to free the Chinook."

"You and Weasel have the strongest jaws," said the boy. "If you each grab hold of the bag and pull as hard as you can, you may be able to tear the bag open."

Coyote and Weasel tried, but the elk skin was too strong. Next, Owl and Magpie took turns trying to peck holes in the bag, but with no success. Then the boy tried to untie the bag, but his fingers were too clumsy.

They were all out of ideas. Just then, a timid prairie chicken approached the group.

"I don't mean to interfere," said Prairie Chicken, "but I may be able to help. I think I can unpick the stitches with my sharp beak."

The friends agreed, and they each held
their breath while Prairie Chicken worked at
unpicking the stitches. Finally, the stitches
came undone and the bag opened. With a
mighty whooshing sound, the Chinook escaped.

Prairie Chicken stepped back, feeling awkward that she had succeeded where the others had failed. But the animals gathered around to congratulate her. "I think I speak for everyone when I say thank you for helping us free the Chinook," said Owl.

Bear was furious when he found that the Chinook was gone. "Now I will never be able to keep my den warm in winter," he said. "I might as well sleep through until spring." And from then on, that's what he did.

As the Chinook blew down from the mountains, the heavy blanket of snow that covered the land began to melt. The sky above the land cleared, forming a great arch of blue sky. The elders knew that their long wait was over, and the Chinook wind was on its way.

The boy and his animal friends made their way back down the mountain with the warm wind at their backs. They each planned what they would do next.

"There will be plenty of mice for me to catch now that the snow is melting," said Owl.

"Not if I catch them first," said Weasel.

"I am quite fond of mice myself," said Coyote.

"I can't wait to tell the story of our adventures," said Magpie.

"Won't you all come home with me first," said the boy. "I'd like to introduce you to my people."

When the boy arrived back home, everyone was celebrating.

"We can't thank you enough for what you have done," said one of the elders.

"I had plenty of help and cooperation from my friends," said the boy.

Summarize

Use details from the story to summarize *The Bear Who Stole the Chinook*. Your chart may help you.

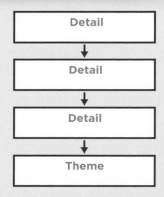

Text Evidence

1. How can you tell this story is a folktale? Identify one feature that tells you this. GENRE

2. Why is the boy working with the animals rather than with the people in his tribe? THEME

3. What does the word *succeeded* on page 12 mean? Use clues in the sentence to find out. ANTONYMS

4. What is the message of *The Bear Who Stole the Chinook*? Write a paragraph about your ideas using details from the text. WRITE ABOUT READING

Compare Texts
Read about how students worked together with their community to help save jobs.

Saving Lubec

The small town of Lubec, Maine, once had a thriving fishing industry. Fishing boats brought in small fish called herring. The herring were processed into sardines in the town's many sardine factories. But by the late 1990s, it had become difficult for the people of Lubec to make a living from the sea. There were not as many herring to be caught. At the same time, Americans were not buying as many sardines. Almost all of the sardine factories closed down.

The fishing town of Lubec is located on the coast of Maine.

Students from Lubec Consolidated School worked on aquaculture projects in Lubec.

In 1995, a group of Lubec high school students and their teacher held a town meeting. They thought aquaculture might help their community. Aquaculture is the farming of fish and water plants. With the help of teachers and townspeople, the students turned an old water-treatment plant near their school into an aquaculture center. The students began to learn about fish farming. They learned how to raise fish in tanks.

(t) © Mike Pietrak

From Fish Tank to Food

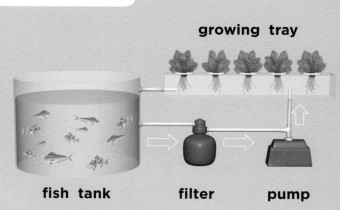

Waste water from fish tanks is filtered and pumped to a greenhouse. This waste water is used to grow vegetables for the school cafeteria.

growing tray

fish tank   filter   pump

The students carried out experiments to see if Lubec could start to sell new types of fish products. They tried out different diets for sea urchins and found that some foods caused the sea urchins to produce more roe. This discovery was good news, as sea urchin roe is very popular in Japan.

sea urchin roe

Sea urchin roe is a Japanese delicacy.

Businesses in Lubec are now making money from the aquaculture projects. More and more students in the town are getting involved in aquaculture. Working together with their community, Lubec's students are helping to create a better future for their town.

Make Connections

In *Saving Lubec*, how has working with their community been good for the students and their school? ESSENTIAL QUESTION

Why is working together a good way to solve a problem? Use examples from *The Bear Who Stole the Chinook* and *Saving Lubec* to support your response. TEXT TO TEXT

Focus on Genre

Folktales Folktales are stories passed on from one person to the next by word of mouth or by oral tradition. Folktales are not realistic. They can include talking animals. Many folktales have a message or a lesson.

Read and Find *The Bear Who Stole the Chinook* is a version of a Siksika Indian folktale. The story teaches about working together. It also gives information about the Siksika Indians, also known as the Blackfeet. The Siksika live in the northern Plains of America and would have experienced the warm winds of the Chinook in the winter. The author has retold this traditional story in her own words.

Your Turn

When someone retells a folktale, they tell the main story using their own words. Choose a folktale you know. Make a flow chart to keep track of the main events. Using the chart to help you, rewrite the folktale in your own words.